THE RED HAT OF KNOWLEDGE

The True Story of El Hadj Saad
Oumar Toure in the Niger Valley

Mahamadou Saad Toure
& Hawa Toure

BabouConnect Publishing

Copyright © [2025] Mahamadou Saad Toure & Hawa Toure

All rights reserved.

No part of this book may be reproduced, stored in a retrieval system, or transmitted in any form or by any means—electronic, mechanical, photocopying, recording, or otherwise—without the prior written permission of the publisher, except in the case of brief quotations embodied in critical reviews and certain other noncommercial uses as permitted by copyright law.

Published by: **BabouConnect Publishing**

["Printed in [USA]"]

ISBN: 979-8-9939072-9-1

For permissions, inquiries, or bulk orders, contact:
[sabilfalah@gmail.com]

This is a work of nonfiction. The events and figures depicted are based on historical facts, author research, and firsthand accounts. Any errors or omissions are unintentional.

First Edition: [2025]

To every **child** who dares to **dream,**
and to the **fathers** who pass on the light.

Contents

Introduction..xi

CHAPTER I: Early Childhood..1

CHAPTER II: Challenges—French School..3

CHAPTER III: Trade and New Skills...7

CHAPTER IV: Father's Trust..9

CHAPTER V: From a Shop to a Classroom...11

CHAPTER VI: Community Resistance and Trust.................................13

CHAPTER VII: A Dream Fulfilled..15

CHAPTER VIII: Final Tribute...17

*In memory of **El Hadj Saad Oumar Toure**,*

*a visionary from West Africa, whose **journey of knowledge***

still inspires hearts across generations.

Map of Ségou, Mali in West Africa — A City of Knowledge Along the Niger River

A Young Saad sits by the Niger River, looking thoughtful, while a few village children in the background play or read Quranic slates.

Introduction:

In the heart of **West Africa**, in the village of **Dougounikoro, Ségou, Mali**, a child was born who would one day **change the way his people learned**. That child was **Saad**. His father, **Oumar**, was a respected **scholar in Islamic studies,** known for his deep understanding of **poetry and literature**. His mother, a woman of **resilience and wisdom**, raised him with patience and strength, teaching him the values of **hard work and perseverance**. From a young age, Saad was **curious**. He loved to listen to the **recitations of elders** and ponder the words they spoke. He observed the world around him, always asking **big questions**. "Why does the wind whisper through the trees? Why can't every child go to school?" Even as a little boy, he made a **silent promise** to himself—one day, he would **change this**.

Saad and a group of children sitting under a tree at night, listening to the village elders teach the Quran, with a lantern softly glowing.

CHAPTER I

Early Childhood:

Every evening, Saad joined a group of six other children to **study the Quran with the village elders.** They sat close together, sharing food and laughter under the soft glow of lanterns. His father, Oumar, often guided them, not only teaching **Quranic verses** but also weaving **poetry and literature** into their lessons. Saad marveled at the **beauty of language and storytelling**, absorbing every lesson with **fascination**. When Saad returned home, his mind buzzed with questions. "Why do we learn this way?" he asked his mother as he helped sweep the yard. "What if one day, I could help more children learn together?" His mother smiled, recognizing the **spark of something special** in her son. "Then, my child," she said, "you must always **seek knowledge** and **never stop learning**."

Saad nervously entering a French classroom for the first time, seeing desks, books, and a teacher writing on a blackboard

CHAPTER II

Challenges: French School

By the time Saad was still a young boy, he had already **memorized one-fourth of the Quran**. His parents were proud of his dedication. But one day, **French officials** arrived in the village and told Saad he had to attend their **school**. "Why do I need to go there?" he wondered. The **French school** was different—**new words**, **new books**, and **unfamiliar rules**. But Saad, always **curious and determined**, decided he would **learn everything he could**. Saad's father deeply valued **tradition**. "No French books in this house!" he would say. "And no French words!" Saad respected his father, but French school introduced him to ideas that **fascinated** him. One day, without thinking, he said, "Oui," instead of "Yes." His father was **furious** and punished him. But Saad didn't give up. He **studied quietly, listening carefully** to his teachers and **memorizing his lessons**. He was determined to make sense of **both worlds**.

Even with the challenges, Saad **excelled at school**. While most children took six years to finish their studies, Saad completed it in just **four**. He was always at the **top of his class**, impressing his teachers with his **sharp mind and hard work**. When he finished sixth grade, he felt a **mix of emotions**. He was proud, but he also thought about his father. "Maybe one day, he'll see that this **knowledge can help our people**," Saad thought.

Saad in a busy marketplace, holding fabric, while merchants and customers barter around him.

CHAPTER III

Trade and New Skills:

After finishing school, Saad's aunt, **Zeynab**, invited him to join her in her **trading business**. Together, they traveled to nearby towns and even across borders, buying and selling goods like **fabric, spices, and livestock**. The bustling markets fascinated Saad. People from all walks of life gathered, exchanging goods and stories. Saad became skilled at **negotiating fair prices** and **managing supplies**. But what he loved most was **meeting new people and learning from them**. On long journeys from Mali to Niger, he carried goods to trade, but he also carried something else—his **thirst for knowledge**. While others were busy counting coins, Saad taught himself to **sew**, stitching fabrics into **fine clothes**. At night, by the light of a small lamp, he **read books about geography and math**. But he had a **secret mission**—he carefully **translated what he learned into Arabic**, making it easier for others in his community to understand.

Saad sitting next to his father, reading a letter aloud while his father listens intently.

CHAPTER IV

Father's Trust:

By the time Saad was eighteen, his father, **Oumar**, began receiving important **letters and telegrams in French**, but he couldn't read them. One evening, he handed Saad a crinkled letter and said, "Saad, read this for me." Saad's heart raced. He carefully unfolded the letter and began **reading aloud**, translating each word into **Arabic**. The room fell silent as the family listened. When he finished, Oumar looked at his son with **pride**. "Your journey with French was not wasted," his father said. From that day on, Saad became the family's **translator**, proving that **knowledge could bridge the gap between two worlds**.

Saad sewing in his small shop, while a few elderly men sit nearby, listening as he teaches them Quranic verses.

CHAPTER V

From a Shop to a Classroom

After earning his father's trust, Saad opened a **small shop** beside their home. The shop was filled with **colorful fabrics** and the rhythmic sound of his **sewing machine**. From morning till evening, he tailored clothes for the community. But when the sun set, his shop transformed into something else—a **place of learning**. Elderly neighbors gathered under the glow of lanterns as Saad patiently **taught them verses from the Quran**. Even after a long day of work, he found joy in **sharing knowledge**, weaving not just clothes, but **bonds of faith and understanding**. As Saad's family grew, so did his **dreams**. When his eldest daughter reached preschool age, he imagined a place where children could **learn together**. One sunny morning, he gathered the neighborhood children and opened his **first Quran school**. With mats laid out and the soft hum of young voices, the journey of **Sébil Falah** had begun.

Parents and elders watching from a distance as Saad teaches children using small tables and a wooden board.

CHAPTER VI

Community Resistance and Trust:

Saad's Quran school was **different**. Instead of sitting on the ground, students used **tables and chairs**, and he introduced a **wooden board for writing**. Some elders were alarmed. "He's trying to change our children," they whispered. "He'll turn them away from tradition!" Saad, undeterred, invited families to visit. "These tools do not change your **faith**," he explained. "They **strengthen your learning**." Slowly, the community saw the results. Children read the **Quran with confidence**, and parents grew proud. Each year, **Sébil Falah expanded**. Saad's students didn't just **memorize verses**—they **understood them**. He introduced a bold idea: **weekly public recitations**, where one student read aloud, and another translated. At first, people watched from a distance. Then, they listened. Then, they **believed**. With trust built, the **school flourished**. Adults joined **evening classes**. Parents who once doubted Saad now **proudly sent their children** to study. Saad had built more than a school—he had built a **bridge**. Over the years, his **dedication and wisdom** earned him great respect, and he became known as **El Hadj Saad Oumar**.

Sébil Falah school, now a thriving institution with students and teachers engaging in lessons

CHAPTER VII

A Dream Fulfilled:

The days of **memorizing on wooden slates** had transformed into a **full educational system**. Saad's students received **scholarships** to study around the world, bringing back **knowledge to their community**. What started as **one small class** had grown into a **legacy of faith and learning**. Through **dedication and wisdom**, El Hadj Saad Oumar Toure had proven that **knowledge**, when shared with **love and purpose**, could **change lives forever**.

Sébil Falah, founded in 1946, became the heart of knowledge in Ségou. This building, erected in 1981, still echoes the footsteps of Saad's dream.

CHAPTER VIII

Final Tribute:

Sébil Falah, built in 1981, became more than a school — it became the beating heart of Saad's dream.

Each wall echoed with the voices of students learning with purpose and teachers guiding with love.

Under Saad's care, it stood not only for knowledge, but for dignity, faith, and determination.

Generations grew within its walls, shaped by his values and inspired by his mission.

Today, Sébil Falah remains a living legacy — a home of learning where Saad's light still shines.

The Niger Valley, West Africa